FRONTIER WOMEN
Who Helped Shape the American West

Ryan P. Randolph

PowerKids Press
New York

To my wife, Joanne, with love

Published in 2003 by The Rosen Publishing Group, Inc.
29 East 21st Street, New York, NY 10010

First Edition

Managing Editor: Kathy Kuhtz Campbell
Book Designer: Emily Muschinske

Photo Credits: Cover and title page, pp. 5, 13 (left) 14 Nebraska State Historical Society, RG2608.PH:1053, RG2608.PH:1309, 1975.11.112, RG2026; back cover, p. 6 (inset left) Fred Hulstrand History in Pictures Collection/NDIRS-NDSU, Fargo; p. 6 (center) © Granger Collection; p. 6 (foreground right) The Society of California Pioneers; p. 9 Whitman Mission National Historic Site; p. 9 (inset) Museum of History and Industry, Seattle; p. 10 Wyoming State Archives Department of State Parks and Cultural Resources; p. 10 (inset) courtesy of Lane County Historical Society; p. 13 (right) courtesy of the California History Room, California State Library, Sacramento California; p. 17 courtesy of the Toledo Ursuline Convent Archives; p. 17 (inset) courtesy Denver Public Library, Western History Collection X-21849; p. 18 © Wyoming Division of Cultural Resources/AP/Wide World Photos; p. 21 courtesy of the National Anthropological Archives, Smithsonian Institution; p. 22 Elmer E. Rasmuson Library, University of Alaska, Fairbanks.

Manufactured in the United States of America

Contents

From the East to the West

When we think about the westward expansion of the United States during the 1800s, images of men as pioneers, cowboys, or gunfighters might come to mind. However, women played important roles on the western frontier.

From 1804 to 1806, explorers Meriwether Lewis and William Clark journeyed from St. Louis, Missouri, to the Pacific Ocean. They depended on a Shoshone woman, Sacagawea, to act as an **interpreter**.

From the 1840s to the 1860s, many women traveled on the Oregon and California Trails. They came to the West to set up homes, farms, and businesses. Until the early 1900s, women of many **ethnic groups** and their families settled the land between the Mississippi River and the Pacific Ocean.

Many women traveled with their families to the West. This 1886 photo shows a family in front of a sod house in Custer County, Nebraska. Called a soddy, a sod house was made from blocks of grass that were laid like bricks. It took only one week to build a 24-foot-long (7-m-long) soddy.

Top Left: *A pioneer family in North Dakota has gathered for a child's funeral. Children often did not live to become teenagers.*

Bottom Right: *Nancy Kelsey was the first white woman to cross the peaks of the Sierra Nevada.*

Left: Narcissa Whitman worked with the Cayuse at Waiilatpu in the Walla Walla Valley of today's Washington State. She taught them about Christianity and about farming crops for themselves.

Bottom Right: These Cayuse twins were photographed in 1898.

Mrs. Smith And
killed Near C[...]
Smith Ph[...]

A Hard, New World

Even after the long trip to the West ended, life in a new home on the frontier was difficult. The diaries and journals of the women on the frontier describe life as lonely and tiring. The physical labor of growing crops and caring for animals was hard, and the hot summers and the cold winters could ruin crops. Families often struggled just to stay alive.

In the early days of frontier settlement, a woman had to help with the farming and the building of a house. She also had to do other work, such as caring for children, cooking, making clothes, and cleaning.

Far Left: Women on the frontier had to make much of their own clothing and supplies. This woman in Oregon is making soap around the year 1908. Left: A frontier woman had to do jobs she might not have to perform back east. This woman with a rifle had to shoot a wildcat in Wyoming.

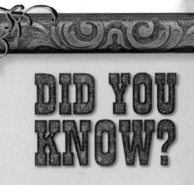

DID YOU KNOW?

The first frontier homes in which families lived were very small. On the plains, one-room houses were often made of sod blocks, sometimes called Nebraska marble. Log cabins could be built in Oregon or California, where trees grew.

Nellie Cashman, the Miner's Angel

Many people traveled to the West to search for gold and silver. Most of these people were men, but there were many women who sought their own fortunes. One such woman was Nellie Cashman, who was known as the Miner's Angel.

Nellie was born around 1845, in Ireland. She journeyed to the American West in the 1860s, and became a cook in the silver mining camps of Nevada. In 1872, she opened a **boardinghouse** with the money she had saved working as a cook. She went to Cassiar, a goldfield in British Columbia, Canada, and in 1874, set up another boardinghouse there. Nellie also went to Tucson and then to Tombstone, Arizona. She opened restaurants, and she fed and cared for miners who were down on their luck. She continued to travel to mining towns until she died in 1925.

Far Right: *Women have brought lunches to some miners in the goldfields of Auburn Ravine, California, in this 1852 photograph. Some women tried their luck in the mining fields. Others made their fortunes by opening businesses, such as restaurants.*

Left: Nellie Cashman was known for her generous nature. She once traveled 77 days in deep snow to bring supplies to help save some sick miners. She was also daring. During the Klondike gold rush, she ran a dogsled team across the Yukon for 750 miles (1,207 km).

Doctor Susan La Flesche Picotte

Native Americans faced many hardships as white settlers moved west. Susan La Flesche Picotte overcame these challenges and was the first Native American woman to become a doctor. She was born in 1865, on the Omaha **reservation** in northern Nebraska. Susan earned her medical degree at Women's Medical College in Pennsylvania in 1889.

Until 1893, Susan worked as a government doctor on the Omaha reservation. She tried to improve **sanitation** and health education. She also worked to build a hospital, which opened in 1913. When Susan died in 1915, the hospital was named for her.

Susan had a dream to build a hospital on the reservation in Walthill, Nebraska. In 1915, a 39-room hospital was named the Dr. Susan La Flesche Picotte Memorial Hospital.

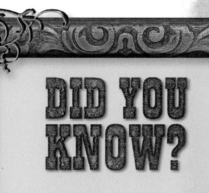

DID YOU KNOW?

Susan La Flesche Picotte was the daughter of Joseph La Flesche, called Iron Eye, a chief of the Omaha, and Mary Gale, called One Woman, who was of the Iowa Nation. In 1894, Susan married Henry Picotte and later had two children.

Stagecoach Mary

Many black women journeyed to the West to find a better life. Although black women still faced **discrimination** on the frontier, many played important roles in churches and government. Many ran restaurants, hotels, and laundry services.

Mary Fields was born into slavery in Tennessee in 1832, and gained her freedom after the **Civil War** (1861–1865). She moved to Cascade, Montana, and worked for the nuns at St. Peter's Mission, helping to build a school. Mary was a strong, hardworking woman. She carried a gun and wore a dress and an apron over men's pants. Mary was fired from St. Peter's after having a gunfight with a man in 1895. She got a job driving a stagecoach to deliver the U.S. mail. She delivered the mail until she was 70 and never missed a day. The townspeople fondly called her Stagecoach Mary. She opened restaurants, a laundry service, and a baby-sitting service before she died in 1914.

Top Right: *The stagecoach was used to carry people, money, and other goods over bumpy trails. These stagecoaches were often targets for robbers.*

Left: *Mary Fields became a stagecoach driver in 1895. Driving a U.S. mail coach was a risky job, but Mary and her gun were more than a match for any danger!*

Esther Hobart Morris lived in South Pass City, in Wyoming Territory. She heard 70 cases as the first female justice of the peace in the United States.

Esther Hobart Morris, Justice of the Peace

Esther Hobart Morris was an important figure in the women's **suffrage** movement. In 1869, Esther and her second husband, John Morris, moved to Wyoming Territory. In 1869, Wyoming became the first territory or state to allow women the right to vote. In 1870, Esther became the first woman in the world to serve as a **justice of the peace**. She served as a judge in the courts of South Pass City in Wyoming for almost nine months. Esther Hobart Morris remained active in the women's rights movement until her death in 1902. In 1960, Wyoming chose a sculpture of Esther to represent the state in Statuary Hall in the U.S. Capitol in Washington, D.C.

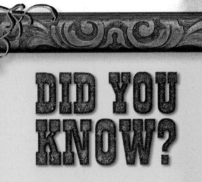

DID YOU KNOW?

Not all women obeyed the laws of the West. Some women were famous outlaws. Pearl Hart was a well-known stagecoach robber in Arizona. Belle Starr was a cattle and horse rustler and was called the Bandit Queen.

Alice Fletcher and Native American Culture

Alice Fletcher was an **anthropologist** and a leader in the movement to have Native Americans accepted in white communities. She began to study Native American anthropology at the Peabody Museum in Cambridge, Massachusetts, in 1880.

In 1881, she moved to Nebraska to live with and study the Omaha. Her studies led her to support **allotment.** In the effort to **assimilate**, or absorb, Native Americans into white culture, tribal lands were broken into plots that individuals could own. Instead of helping Native Americans to assimilate, allotment enabled Native American lands to be sold to white settlers. The practice of allotment helped to destroy the Native American way of life, although this is not what Alice had aimed to do.

Alice worked to save the culture of the Omaha and other Native American nations. In 1890, she wrote several books about the people and the cultures that she had studied.

Below: *Alice Fletcher was born in Cuba in 1838, but soon moved to New York. As an anthropologist, she helped to save the music, the dances, the religion, and the culture of the Omaha, Nez Percé, Sioux, and Pawnee. By the time she died in 1923, she helped to found the American Anthropological Association and other scientific groups.*

The Legacy of Frontier Women

Women were just as important as men were in settling the American West. It was the presence of men, women, and their children that helped to bring law and order to the frontier. As more families moved to the West, the number of schools, sheriffs, judges, and government services also increased.

The women who first traveled on the westward trails saw even more pioneers move to the West in the late 1860s, when railroads crossed the country. By 1890, so many people had moved to the American frontier that the government called it closed. The **legacy** of the women who helped to shape the American West will live on as long as we remember their exciting adventures.

Around 1900, this woman was photographed with miners in the goldfields of Alaska.

Glossary

allotment (uh-LAHT-muhnt) Tribal lands that are divided into smaller plots so that each person receives an individual plot to own.

anthropologist (an-thruh-PAH-luh-jist) A person who studies the behavior or culture of people.

assimilate (uh-SIH-muh-layt) To absorb, or blend into, the cultural tradition of a group of people.

boardinghouse (BOR-ding-hows) A house for lodging where meals are served.

Civil War (SIH-vul WOR) The war fought between the Northern and Southern states of America from 1861 to 1865.

discrimination (dis-krih-muh-NAY-shun) Treating a person badly or unfairly just because he or she is different.

economic depression (eh-kuh-NAH-mik dih-PREH-shuhn) A period of low buying and selling of goods and services.

ethnic groups (ETH-nik GROOPS) Groups of people having the same race, culture, or language, or belonging to the same country.

interpreter (in-TER-pruh-ter) A person who explains the meaning of one language with another.

justice of the peace (JUS-tis UV THUH PEES) A judge who acts on lower court cases and who can perform marriages and other official tasks.

legacy (LEH-guh-see) Something of value that one generation leaves for the next.

missionaries (MIH-shuh-ner-eez) People who are sent to do religious work in a territory or a foreign country.

reservation (reh-zer-VAY-shun) A piece of public land set aside for Native Americans to live on.

sanitation (sa-nih-TAY-shun) The act of using measures, such as cleanliness, that protect public health. The disposing of sewage.

suffrage (SUH-frij) The right of voting.

Index

Primary Sources

Front Cover and title page. *Chrisman Sisters.* An 1886 photo shows the Chrisman sisters, Harriet, Elizabeth, Lucie, and Ruth, on their claim in Goheen settlement on Lieban Creek (also known as Lillian Creek) in Custer County, Nebraska. **Back cover.** *A Frontier Woman with Her Horses.* This woman is seen in front of a sod house in South Dakota around 1900. **Page 5.** *A Group of Women, a Man, and Horses in Front of a Sod House.* This photo was taken in 1886, near Ansley in Custer County, Nebraska. **Page 6.** *Emigrants Travel on a Wagon Train in the Sierra Nevada in California.* This 1866 photo shows a group of people journeying through Strawberry Valley in California. **Page 6 (top left).** *A Funeral.* A family had this picture taken to document the death of a child in the first decade of the 1900s. The location is probably somewhere in North Dakota. **Page 6 (bottom right).** *Nancy Kelsey.* This undated photo is now in the collection of the Society of California Pioneers. **Page 9 (left).** *Narcissa Prentiss Whitman.* Drury Haight based this painting of Mrs. Whitman on a sketch by Paul Kane. Kane was known to have drawn a portrait of Mrs. Whitman. Haight's and Kane's portraits have been published in Clifford M. Drury's *Marcus and Narcissa Whitman and the Opening of Old Oregon*, a two-volume history of the Whitman Mission in Walla Walla, Washington. **Page 9 (right).** *Cayuse Twins in Cradleboards.* An 1898 photo by Lee Moorhouse shows the Cayuse twins, Tax-a-Lax and Alompum, who were the grandnieces of Chief Joseph. The twins lived in northeastern Oregon. Moorhouse, an Oregon pioneer and a government agent of Native American affairs on the Umatilla Reservation, became a photographer in 1897. **Page 10 (left).** *Mrs. Smith and Wildcat She Killed Near Glenrock, Wyoming.* This photo is now in the collection of the Wyoming State Archives. **Page 13 (left).** *Nellie Cashman.* Nellie was also known as the Angel of Tombstone because of her works of charity in that Arizona town. This undated portrait of Cashman is now in the collection of the Arizona Historical Society. **Page 17 (top right).** *Men and a Woman on a Stagecoach.* Men and a woman are seen here sometime between 1880 and 1900, riding on a stagecoach in Routt County, Colorado. **Page 17 (left).** *Mary Fields.* Stagecoach Mary is seen here with her rifle and dog. The photo is in the collection of Sister Mary Rose Krupp, Ursuline Convent Offices, in Toledo, Ohio.

Web Sites

Due to the changing nature of Internet links, PowerKids Press has developed an online list of Web sites related to the subject of this book. This site is updated regularly. Please use this link to access the list:

www.powerkidslinks.com/lwe/frwomen/